OUR G... IS BROKE!

MW01225706

Solution: Invoke Article V of the Constitution.

STEVE HESS is a retired CPA and Chief Financial Officer for several Silicon Valley companies. He was involved in raising venture capital, bank financing, long-term strategic planning, initial public offerings, and mergers and acquisitions.

ISBN: 9798530109393

CONTENTS

INTRODUCTION

Currently, the federal government's debt is $28 trillion and is expected to grow to over $40 trillion by 2026. This is a financial crisis that will not be resolved by the U.S. Congress. Congress is unwilling and unable to take action to stop the run-away spending, and annual deficits of over $1.5 trillion. In 2020, interest on the government's debt was $371 billion and is forecasted to be as much as $768 billion in 2026. That's right; the interest expense could more than double in five years!

The White House and Congress continue to do nothing about the upcoming crisis. Unless there is a drastic change in the way our government operates, this is what we can expect:

- The government will keep spending more than it takes in from taxes.
- The national debt will grow by over $1.5 trillion per year.
- Annual Interest expense will soar.
- Income taxes will increase.
- While the current money supply is at record levels, the Federal Reserve will continue bailing out the government by printing more money.
- We will see hyperinflation and the dollar will be worth much less.

- Next, the Federal Reserve will increase interest rates to tame inflation.
- Higher interest rates and higher taxes will cause the economy to faulter, and we will have a deep, long recession.
- Then, in order to jump start the economy, the government will (in their infinite wisdom) create more spending programs and print more money.
- Buyers of government debt (Treasury securities) will lose confidence in Uncle Sam's ability to repay it.
- The bond rating agencies will downgrade U.S. Treasuries causing interest rates to increase even more.
- The stock and bond markets will be in turmoil.

Get the picture? This vicious cycle will continue until it becomes obvious that the U.S. government is bankrupt.

To make matters worse, while the government's debt stands at $28 trillion, this does not include its commitment to fund future Social Security and other entitlements to the tune of $96 trillion. It's not so much of a stretch of the imagination to see that the U.S. government won't be able to meet all of its future financial obligations.

Don't think bankruptcy could happen? Over the last 200 years, 83 countries have gone bankrupt. Here are some high-profile bankruptcies caused by financial mismanagement in the last 90 years:

- Venezuela 2018
- City of Detroit 2013
- Greece 2009
- General Motors, AIG, & Leman Bros. 2009
- Argentina 2001
- Russia 1998
- Mexico 1982
- New York City 1975
- United Kingdom 1931

In addition to the government's financial problems, it is becoming more and more obvious that Washington DC wants to be involved in every aspect of our lives. The Constitution clearly limits the purpose of the federal government: protect our boarders, defend us from war, negotiate with foreign countries, regulate interstate commerce, and taxation.

Washington's problems are not the sole responsibility of the Democrats, Republicans, conservatives or liberals. Congress as a body is totally dysfunctional. Both parties are focused on re-election and grabbing power.

When the founders drafted the Constitution, they knew there would be a time when the federal government would become too powerful and over-reaching, leading to tyranny. As an answer to this concern, they included Article V which allows the states to call a convention in order to develop an appropriate remedy, and amend the Constitution.

Here's the good news. There is already a movement afoot with the states to use Article V to do these three things:
1. Force Congress to balance the budget.
2. Create term limits.
3. Limit the federal government's jurisdiction over the states.

In order to invoke Article V, 34 states (each having one vote) must approve it within their own state legislatures and file an application with Congress. Next, there will be a <u>Convention of States,</u> at which time the language for the amendment will be crafted. Following that, the proposed amendment goes out to the 50 states for a final vote. If 38 of the states vote for passage of the proposed amendment, it becomes law and Congress must abide by it.

However, this process needs to move more rapidly because frankly, time is not on our side.

This is our last chance to avoid a financial crisis!

To give you an appreciation of the size of the problem, here is what the unabbreviated debt looks like:

$28,000,000,000,000

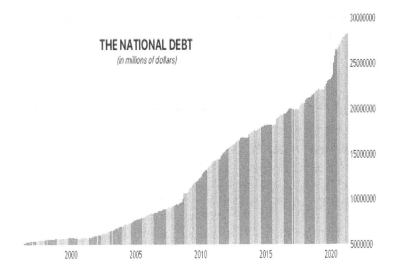

THE NATIONAL DEBT
(in millions of dollars)

As Congress continues to avoid dealing with this daunting challenge, they have not warned us of the consequences that will have far reaching effects on our nation's financial viability. This is a horrible debt to be passing on to our children and grandchildren!

Some issues that may make things even more desperate:

- China currently holds $1.2 trillion of our treasury securities. Our annual trade deficits with China are running over $300 billion. What if they (and /or other foreign countries) start dumping Treasuries in the open market driving their value down significantly?

- Any rumors that the U.S. is having problems servicing (or reducing) its debt will have broad implications, that include a more difficult environment for the U.S. to sell Treasuries at reasonable interest rates, or at all.

- We have no financial safety net in the event we encounter another widespread tragedy such as Covid 19.

Today's situation reminds me of the financial crisis of 2008 and the Great Recession. The mortgage financing industry wrote too many mortgages for home purchases to people that were not credit worthy; many of whom couldn't even make their car payments, let alone a mortgage payment. The problem grew into a gigantic balloon that finally popped and blind-sided nearly everyone. The government's debt problem has now reached 'fully-inflated status'!

In all of this, the Congressional Budget Office (the 'CBO') which reports the government's financial results to Congress, continues to sound the alarm only to fall on deaf ears, as Congress goes 'whistling past the graveyard'. My plea is for immediate action by states leadership to make the big, bold, changes desperately needed by invoking Article V, NOW!

The purpose of this book is to raise the awareness of how wasteful spending and mismanagement has caused an accumulation of extreme debt, that will significantly damage our economy. **It is therefore a call to action for Americans to communicate with their state representatives and tell them to vote in favor of a Convention of States under Article V.** Help them understand that a Constitutional amendment is the only way our federal government can get bailed out.

American's need to know about this situation

The fact of the matter is that the majority of us don't have a lot of spare time to research the government's finances to see if they're in trouble. We work hard at our jobs. We try to make ends meet. We have kids to raise. In any event, <u>here we are today with the potential tragic loss of our world position as the wealthiest nation,</u> and your U.S. representatives probably haven't told you about it.

If you're fed-up with our dysfunctional government; if you stopped watching network news because it's too depressing; and, if you feel like you're ready to take action, please take some time to spread the word about this 'now-or-never' opportunity to head off the pending final crisis. This may well be the fight of our lives.

AN OVER-REACHING, BLOATED GOVERNMENT

Many Americans know that the federal government is a dysfunctional and wasteful giant that wants to control most every aspect of our lives. There are trillions of dollars sloshing around in the various bureaucracies, and of course, it's what you call OPM – (other peoples' money). It really makes most angry to see taxpayer money wasted.

Alan Greenspan is an economist that spent five terms as the Federal Reserve Chairman. He was once asked if Congress wastes money to intentionally collapse our economy. He said, "I don't think so. Government spending is an addiction". It's not surprising that in a June 2021 Gallup poll, 26% of Americans said they approved of how Congress handles things, while 71% disapproved.

Scholarly studies support the idea that many federal activities are misguided and harmful. A book titled *Why Government Fails So Often,* by Yale University law professor Peter Schuck put it this way: "From healthcare to workplace conduct, the federal government is taking on ever more responsibility for managing our lives. The most alarming consequence of ineffective policies, in addition to unrealized social goals, is the growing threat to the government's democratic legitimacy".

In his book, Schuck provides a wide range of examples and an enormous body of evidence to explain why so many domestic policies go awry, because of deep structural flaws that undermine every administration – Democratic and Republican. Recurring weaknesses include unrealistic goals, perverse incentives, poor and distorted information, lack of credibility, and shocking financial waste.

The General Accounting Office (the GAO), is often called the "congressional watchdog". It's an independent, non-partisan agency that works for Congress. One of their principle jobs is to audit government spending. I'm going to give you a tiny sample of some of the egregious waste they have uncovered over time:

- Healthcare fraud is estimated to cost $60 billion a year.
- $200,000 for a tattoo removal program.
- The federal government owns and maintains 50,000 vacant homes
- More than $13 billion in Iraq aid has been classified as wasted or stolen
- 900,000 of the 2.5 million recipients of Katrina assistance provided false names, addresses, or Social Security numbers.
- Congress ignored efficiency

recommendations from the Department of Health and Human Services that would have saved $9 billion annually.

- Audits showed $34 billion worth of Department of Homeland Security contracts contained significant waste, fraud, and abuse.
- $968,932 spent on developing a master's degree in research ethics in Myanmar.
- Washington made a $2 billion 'investment' in a company by the name of Solyndra which shortly thereafter went bankrupt.
- $1.3 million to study whether people will eat ground-up bugs
- $3.45 million to send messages to mothers, to encourage their teenage daughters to stop indoor tanning
- $2 million for testing if using a hot tub can lower stress
- The eight Ivy League colleges have received grants of $9.8 billion from government, despite having a collective endowment of $140 billion.
- $200 billion in duplicative federal programs, agencies, offices, and initiatives.

Career politicians are dangerous

President Biden recently signed a sweeping new executive order aimed at cracking down on anti-competitive behaviour by 'big tech', and other industries. Comprised of 72 actions, the order is intended to promote competition in the economy by encouraging more than a dozen federal agencies to scrutinize corporate mergers, and other ways that a growing number of companies build their market power. The order is intended to "reduce the trend of corporate consolidation, increase competition, and deliver concrete benefits to America's consumers, workers, farmers, and small businesses," the White House said.

Recently, a Washington federal judge handed Facebook a victory in its battle against government regulators, dismissing two antitrust lawsuits against the social media company and questioning assertions that Facebook is a monopoly. The judge said the Federal Trade Commission (FTC) had failed to offer enough facts in its complaint to prove its assertions.

There is a very robust legal process in place to evaluate whether a proposed corporate merger creates a monopoly, or is otherwise detrimental to consumers or competition. The FTC relies on the Hart-Scott-Rodino Act of 1976 to make this determination. During this process, companies must prepare filings that describe in great detail their business, markets, competition, financial information, and much more. The filings are processed and analyzed by a team of corporate law professionals representing the companies, and who interact with a team of law professionals at the FTC. It is a time consuming, and intense process. In certain situations, where the proposed merger will affect a great deal of consumers and / or competitors, the process may carry on for a couple of years.

President Biden chose Lina Khan as the new chair of the FTC. She was previously a professor at Columbia Law School and is keen on attacking big technology companies. Ms. Khan is all of 32 years old and has no actual business experience. Her very first assignment is to refile an antitrust complaint against Facebook and convince a federal judge to reconsider the complaint he so expeditiously threw out.

Consider this:
- The FTC has been doing a great job for many years.
- The Justice Department that hears FTC cases has been doing a great job for many years.
- Companies within the high technology industry are fiercely competitive — much to the benefit of consumers.
- Innovation from big tech has created many markets, and millions of jobs.
- Mr. Biden says he wants to protect small companies from big ones. Well, Facebook was a small company not too long ago. The company has grown in value from $0 to almost $1 trillion! This is the story of America and free-trade capitalism. We see new, small companies in technology (and other industries) emerging every day.

My point is that Mr. Biden's 72-point executive order is a creation of more wasteful bureaucracy to fix a problem that doesn't exist. In this particular case, the

FTC, the law, and the judicial process was used effectively, but Mr. Biden didn't like the answer.

While Mr. Biden has a problem with Facebook being too big, he proposed a bill to help the 'big tech' semiconductor industry with a $50 billion grant to build new manufacturing facilities and for research and development. This was in response to the temporary shortage of semiconductors which has caused temporary disruption in other industries including the manufacture of automobiles.

The bill makes no sense. The semiconductor industry has managed its way through cyclical ups and downs for over 45 years with great success. No doubt they will be successful this time as well. After all, in a capitalistic society private companies have a self-interest profit motive, and a strong incentive to succeed. And when the government gives companies money, they don't have an incentive to be efficient with it.

President Biden's real concern should be that Taiwan Semiconductor Inc. (with a $560 billion market value, headquartered in Hsinchu, Taiwan) is now the dominant world manufacturer of semiconductors, at the expense of our U.S. domestic businesses. As Taiwan moves toward re-unification with China, it will be highly connected to the desires of China and its espionage.

The Covid $1.9 trillion financial stimulus

There's no doubt it was a good idea to help people who were hurt financially during the pandemic. But, true to form, the government's handling of the process was inefficient, highly contentious, and not executed well. Checks went out in mass quantities such that people who were high earners and didn't need a check, got them anyway. Unfortunately, these government checks have become a disincentive for people to work. Currently, there are 9.4 million job openings for only 9.0 million people unemployed. Lots of people are getting more money from the government than they would working. No wonder we are currently dealing with supply and distribution problems...

I bet you won't be shocked to know that the $1.9 trillion bill for Covid 19 relief has money set aside for projects that have nothing to do with Covid 19 (a.k.a. Pork):

- $500 million for museums and Native American language preservation.
- $129 billion for K-12 education.
- $40 billion for colleges and universities.
- $7 billion for nutrition assistance for schools.
- $40 billion grants for childcare providers and Head Start.
- $11 billion for human services, labor programs, and other policies.
- $50 million for Planned Parenthood.

- $1.5 billion for Amtrak (even though they still have over a billion dollars from the last grant).
- $1.5 million to repair a bridge connecting Canada and New York.
- $100 million for an underground rail project in Silicon Valley.

The infrastructure bill

In June 2021, the Senate passed a bill for $1.2 trillion to be spent over an eight-year infrastructure' portion of the proposal, here are some of the things that will be included:
- $45 billion for school meals.
- $200 billion toward free "universal, high quality preschool".
- $109 billion for two years of free community college.
- $9 billion in funding to support American teachers.

Since the government doesn't have any money, these infrastructure costs will be paid for by increased taxes from corporations and wealthy people, and by selling more Treasuries to the Fed. Oh, and Congress is going to come up with $70 billion by 'cutting waste and fraud associated with federal spending on unemployment benefits. Why would they wait for something like the infrastructure bill to cut waste and fraud? If the bill doesn't pass, will they just continue wasting $70 billion?

'Obfuscation' helps to get bills passed

Not only have politicians worked hard to confuse taxpayers and load bills with pork, they have also used tactics to confuse each other, thus causing them to sign the bill in order to avoid appearing ignorant. Jack Abramoff, a corrupt Washington lobbyist, went on the 60 Minutes program and confessed he often used a tactic called "obfuscation" to intentionally make a proposed bill so incomprehensible that no one had the time or ability to understand it. The objective was to get members of Congress to vote in favor of the bill, based on verbal assurances rather than having to wade through its voluminous pages.

Can we afford to give billions to other countries?

I don't know much about how foreign aid works, but I know there are many countries that could really benefit from some of our money. However, our government is broke, and it is dubious to think we can continue to give $48 billion a year to other countries. Oh, and we are currently spending $60 million per week ($3.1 billion a year) to shelter unaccompanied minors at the southern border.

Previous attempts to balance the budget have failed

Over the years, there have been efforts by former congressional representatives who have attempted to put wasteful spending in the light of day, in an effort to shame others into cutting the deficits:

- William Proxmire's Golden Fleece award started in 1975 as a tongue-in-cheek gesture. The award was periodically given in recognition of the most outlandish waste of money. The Golden Fleece award was re-launched in 2015 by French Hill (Rep. Arkansas)
- The Bowles Simpson Commission on Fiscal Responsibility and Reform in 2010 was formed to disclose and resolve wasteful spending and reduce deficits. The commission proposed sweeping changes that would reduce deficits by $5 trillion over a 10-year period. Unfortunately, President Obama did not support their recommendations, so the program died.

Others that have put a great deal of effort in trying to reverse the tide of waste include: Senator Tom Coburn; Senator Tim Scott; Representative Paul Ryan (who worked on a bipartisan recommendation on how to save Social Security); Representative Virginia Foxx; and Eric Cantor and his YouCut program. Unfortunately, despite the efforts of these great patriots, wasteful spending has only accelerated over the years.

The tax code is a monstrosity

Most know that our tax code is a mess. Something very ironic is that everyone in Congress agrees, but there's been no progress made on tax reform.

Indeed, it has gotten more and more complex over the years. Here are a few self-indicting quotes from politicians:

- "The income tax code and its associated regulations contain almost 5.6 million words–seven times as many as the Bible. Taxpayers now spend about 5.4 billion hours a year trying to comply with 2,500 pages of tax law." – Rob Portman (R-OH)
- "The Federal tax code with its 44,000 pages, 5.5 million words, and 721 different forms is a patchwork maze of complexity and a testament to confusion over common sense." – Jim DeMint (R-SC)
- "The tax code is a complicated mess. You realize it's a million pages long." – President George W. Bush
- "The current tax code, which at 1.3 million pages, is twice the length of Tolstoy's War and Peace." – Dave Hobson (R-OH)

Former Treasury Secretary Timothy Geithner oversaw, among other things, the IRS. He was caught by an IRS audit that found he owed $34,000 in back taxes. He paid these additional taxes, but this raises a question as to whether he was a cheater, or whether the tax code is so complex that even the guy at the top of the Treasury Department can't figure it out. (Two senior senators investigated the matter and concluded it was an innocent mistake.) The fact of the matter is most accountants, financial planners, and even IRS agents frequently come up with different interpretations of the same tax questions. My brother, my sister-in-law, and I were CPAs before we retired. Because of the increased complexity of the code, we can no longer prepare our own returns.

Many books and white papers have been written about simplifying the tax code. The common thread between those various analyses is that we can greatly simplify the code and collect the same amount of taxes. The key is to close loopholes, broaden the base of taxpayers, and make it fair. One idea is something called the Fair Tax, which is a national sales tax. Instead of paying taxes on the income you receive, you would pay taxes when you buy something. It's simple, fair, and would eliminate the many hours of doing tax returns. If you were a criminal drug dealer and didn't pay income taxes on your $10 million of ill-gotten gains, with the Fair Tax you would pay your fair share of taxes when you purchased your houses, cars, airplanes, and other things. An additional benefit of simplification is the substantial cost savings from eliminating much of the IRS department and tax preparation fees. Tax simplification would eliminate crazy loopholes and the use of taxation as a vote-buying mechanism.

One of the reasons our current code is so convoluted is because politicians have promised to give certain groups tax breaks while increasing taxes on the wealthy to win votes. Rather than tax simplification, President Biden is currently proposing to add $80 billion to the

IRS to accelerate audits on 'high-earners'. This plan assumes greater tax enforcement that will produce $700 billion from cheaters over the next 10 years. To me, this sounds like another government program destined for failure. First, I think high earners are more likely to engage CPAs to prepare their tax returns, and thus lower the chance of errors or fraud. Secondly, we know that because of the incredible complexity of the tax code, any particular issue can be interpreted a number of different ways. Any conflicting interpretation may end up in tax court for a prolonged period of time—thus creating more social and economic waste.

Americans give about $434 billion a year to charities. Given the upcoming increases in taxes on the wealthy, it is likely these contributions will decline. The local schools and charities may be in jeopardy. As the famous clergyman William J. H. Boetcker said "You cannot help the poor by destroying the rich. You cannot strengthen the weak by weakening the strong. You cannot lift the wage earner up by pulling the wage payer down".

How over-regulation hurts the economy

While Congress is composed of members representing the various 50 states as a body, it has this desire to come up with one-size-fits-all solutions to the nation's issues. There are dozens of examples of this, but I'll touch on just a couple.

There is a proposal in Congress called the '2021 Raise the Wage Act', which would raise the minimum wage from $7.25 to $15 per hour by 2025. The 50 states already regulate minimum wages with their own law. It's obvious that wage rates vary significantly depending on local economics. According to Zip Recruiter, the current average hourly pay rate in California (where the cost of living is high) is $30, compared to $16 in Arkansas. We don't need the federal government to help us with this.

One of the best examples of over-regulation is Obamacare. Some 2,700 pages long and full of who knows what. Nancy Pelosi, Democratic House leader, famously stated, "We have to pass the [Obamacare] bill so that we can find out what's in it."

Everyone knows the nation's healthcare system has been a mess for a long time. Americans spend more money on healthcare than any other developed nation in the world, and our outcomes are arguably no better. We spend approximately 18% of our GDP on healthcare, compared to between 8% and 10% for other countries such as Japan, Germany, Sweden, the U.K., and Canada.

The stories are many and well documented regarding what is wrong with our healthcare system. If we could be more efficient, as in the case of our friends abroad, we could save billions of dollars that could be shifted to product innovation, education, new markets, new customers, etc., instead of grossly overpaying to get sick people well.

Obamacare was highly controversial, contentious, and included many issues that seemed misguided, including:

- The IRS was given an extra $500 million to hunt down Americans who were not complying with the bill.
- It imposes new taxes on the American people.
- It limits the treatment options that doctors and patients can consider.
- Nightmarish paperwork burdens.
- If you exercised your right not to have insurance, you had to pay a penalty.
- Healthcare insurance premiums for younger Americans have soared.
- Small businesses are required to provide expensive health insurance for their employees. (Some businesses work around this by firing full-time workers and hiring part-time workers).
- The number of doctors will decline, resulting in a severe shortage.
- Obamacare is universally hated by; the medical profession, corporate CEOs, small business owners, and many members of Congress.

If you are interested in learning how other developed countries are meeting health care needs of their people while incurring half what it costs America, there is a great book written by T.R. Reid titled *The Healing of America – a Global Quest for Cheaper, and Fairer Health Care*. Reid is a long-time correspondent for the Washington Post, has lived in many different countries around the world during his career, and has received health care from those countries.

After reading the book, it was my conclusion that America has the most complex and inefficient healthcare system in the world. A better way would be to adopt best practices from other countries that are succeeding.

The Jones Act of 1920

Government regulations can hurt the economy, especially when they are outdated and should be repealed. The Jones Act of 1920 requires that all ships of cargo from one US port to another be carried on vessels built in the US, owned by a US citizen, and operated by a US crew. Back in 1920 the US shipbuilding industry and labor unions argued that this was needed for national defense and security reasons. Senator John McCain, who was a leading national security hawk, called the reasons for maintaining the Jones Act as "laughable". A GAO study showed that repealing the antiquated Act would save over $656 million a year.

Big governments are not good at running big operations

Another example of big government ineptness is the U.S. Post Office. It is constantly running out of money. In contrast to the ailing Post Office, take a look at two private enterprises which are thriving by delivering mail and packages to the public: Federal Express and UPS.

- FedEx has over $78 billion in annual sales and after-tax profits of over $3 billion. They employ over 180,000 people. The total value of the company's stock is over $78 billion.
- UPS has annual sales of over $89 billion with net income of over $5 billion. They employ over 380,000 people. The total value of UPS stock is over $176 billion.

Both of these companies are successful because they are profit driven. They have shareholders who demand they perform well and provide a good return on their investment. If you have invested in a mutual fund in your 401(k), there is a good chance your fund owns UPS and/or FedEx. These companies are examples of what have made America great and what can be done with unleashed capitalism.

The U.S. DOJ sues Georgia over voting rules

A law signed by Georgia Governor Brian Kemp, requires voters to present identification to request and/or file an absentee ballot, replacing the signature matching processes. It also requires ballot drop boxes in each county, while mandating they are physically secure, and stiffens penalties on 'electioneering' at polling stations. A subsection of the bill purportedly prevents voters in line from being given bottled water. The DOJ's suit alleges Georgia state lawmakers rushed through a sweeping overhaul with an intent to deny Black voters equal access to the ballot.

Georgia Attorney General Chris Carr defended his state's new voting rights law stating, "They [the DOJ] are not upholding the rule of law and this blatantly political lawsuit is legally, factually, and constitutionally wrong. Anybody who looks at our law can see it improves security access, and improves transparency in Georgia's law," he said.

This sort of federal government meddling and harassment has got to stop. Why don't they focus on fixing the antiquated national voting procedure which has dozens of security issues? Here's an idea:

- Utilize the U.S. Social Security Departments master files. Create an 'Eligibility File' that only includes records of U.S. Citizen's (born here, or naturalized) that are still alive, and excludes people below the voting age. There you have it; a file of qualified voters with unique identification numbers – their SS#. When you go to vote you provide your unique identification number and it is matched to the Eligibility File. This helps to make sure everyone gets one, and only one vote, and there is no discrimination.

- Obtain a file from Homeland Security of escaped criminals and non-qualifying felons. Use this file to update the Eligibility File.
- Hire a software team from Silicon Valley to do the work. It will probably take them ten days to complete!

The Deep State (a.k.a. The Swamp)

The Deep State is generally referred to as a body of people, typically influential members of government agencies or the military, believed to be involved in the secret manipulation or control of government policy for personal power and profit. We all know that the Deep State exists and that it grows with the growth of government.

Jason Chaffetz served as the U.S. Rep. for Utah's 3rd congressional district from 2009 until his retirement in 2017. He chaired the Committee on Oversight and Government Reform from 2015 until 2017. That committee was an investigative watch dog of the United States House of Representatives. As Chairman, Jason was primarily responsible for holding Congress accountable. As you can imagine, he witnessed many situations involving abuse of power. After retiring, Jason wrote a book titled *The Deep State* which exposes abuse of power in the out-of-control bureaucracy. I'll touch on just a few examples:

Establishing duplicative or unnecessary bureaucracies is a Deep State specialty

In 2010, Elizabeth Warren, senator from Massachusetts started a new government department entitled Consumer Financial Protection Bureau (CFPB) whose charter was to provide a single point of accountability for enforcing federal consumer financial laws and protecting consumers in the financial marketplace. An organization of unaccountable bureaucrats was created to write more regulations, spend millions, and protect us from ourselves.

The CFPB is funded by the Federal Reserve (the U.S. banking system) and therefore is not accountable to the U.S. Congress. It has more than 1,600 employees that are housed in a building that was built for $139 million and is located in the highest rent district in Washington DC. The construction costs were 300% over budget.
The CFPB spent more than $43 million on public relations and advertising.

It turns out people looking to buy a house can simply stop by the local realtor's office, search Zillow, google for mortgage rates, or search any number of bank websites for the 'consumer protection' provided by the costly services of CFPB.

Lack of accountability is seen all over the Deep State

John Beale agreed to join the EPA in 1989 and received a hiring bonus equal to 25% of his salary. John continued to receive an annual 'hiring bonus' every year for the time he worked for the EPA because no one remembered to stop paying it.

In 2000, John did not show up for work on certain Wednesdays, which he claimed were his "confidential oversight operations meetings". Those meetings amounted to 107 days over a 7-year period. Of course, he was not actually at meetings, he simply took the days off.

In 2008, he did not show up at the office for a period of six months and claimed it was an intense time of confidential meetings in secretive cooperation with the CIA. Nobody bothered to check that story.

On many occasions, John told his employer that he needed to travel to California and charged the EPA a total of $57,000 for travel costs. Turns out he was actually visiting family in Bakersfield.
John claimed he contracted malaria while serving in Vietnam and that he needed a handicap parking slot that costs the government $8,000 to provide. Turns out he was never in Vietnam.

John had a series of supervisors over the years and convinced them he had been directed by the CIA to work on some covert strategies that were so secret he would have to work at home for three years on the project.

In 2011, John retired and was thrown a very lavish retirement party with over 100 in attendance and was praised by all for his great contribution to the EPA and CIA. In the first year that followed his retirement, he was paid his usual salary of $206,000 plus the annual 25% hiring bonus.

John was caught and testified before Congress as to what he had done. He had to repay the government $886,186 before going to jail in 2013. I wonder how many other people like John are employed by our huge government and have never been caught?

Members of the Deep State are above the law

Some years ago, House representative Charlie Rangel was censured by the House Ethics committee for thirteen counts of violation of House rules and federal laws, including tax fraud and using taxpayer money to fund his vacation trips to the Caribbean. Ironically, Mr. Rangel was allowed to continue as a member of the House Ways and Means Committee which oversees federal taxation matters. (Any other US citizen would have been thrown in jail for a long time).

A more highly recognized abuse of power story is the time that Hillary Clinton got a pass from the FBI. While Hillary was Secretary of State, she maintained a server at her home which contained her email correspondence. The State Department never certified the server as secure, as its rules require.

Hillary went before Congress to testify regarding the Benghazi attack of 2012. During inquiries, it became known that she had a private server at home which contained State Department high security communications. She also stated that most of the data on the server had been erased. Wiping the server clean is a violation of The Federal Records Act which states that information and records obtained during her employment belong to the State Department.

Why would Hillary want to keep all her communications as secretary of state on a private server? Possible answer: to avoid complying with various requests filed by the media and the public under the Freedom of Information Act. But if someone has nothing to hide, why hide? Perhaps she wanted to hide decisions and mistakes that would look bad when she ran for president. Or perhaps she wanted to keep from view evidence that she was using her power to enrich herself.

James Comey, then head of the FBI, said that Hillary's actions were just careless, and that the FBI would not be pursuing charges.

Contrast the handling of Hillary's misdeeds to the two-year witch hunt into President Trump's background, spending tens of millions of taxpayer dollars, only to come up empty. During the course of the witch hunt, several bad actors were discovered in the FBI, which was an embarrassment to the department.

HOW GOVERNMENT DEBT AFFECTS OUR ECONOMY

The government issues Treasury bonds in the open market to raise money to cover its deficit spending. This process applies upward pressure on interest rates and inflation. Too much inflation and the Federal Reserve must raise interest rates in order to slow the economy, which in turn reduces inflation. If the economy slows too much it could result in a recession. Piling up more and more government debt is like throwing fuel on the fire.

In order to understand the complexity of these important financial dynamics, please read the following brief tutorial.

#1. It's helpful to know the cast of players who manage the government's finances, banking, and the economy. The Treasury Department is a cabinet position and is responsible for issuing currency and coinage, accounting for the government's tax receipts and expenses, overseeing the Internal Revenue Service, and managing the government's national debt.

The Federal Reserve (the "Fed") is the US banking industry and is independent of the U.S. Government, but is subject to congressional oversight. The Fed regulates the banking system, manages the nation's money supply, and sets interest rate policy in order to help manage the economy.

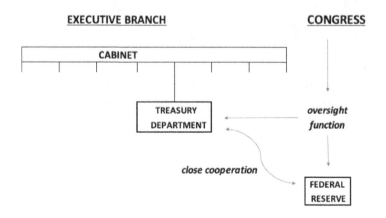

#2 The federal government spends more money than it takes in from taxes. Because of this, it must borrow money by selling government Treasury bonds in the open market. (For now on, I will simply refer to these bonds as Treasuries). Each Treasury is issued by the government at a set face value (ex. $1,000), and a fixed rate of interest (ex. 1.2% which is $12 per year). The owner of that security can hold it to maturity or sell it in the open market for whatever someone is willing to pay. If buyers are feeling good about the government's finances, they might be willing to pay $1,050 for your security. Since the interest of $12/yr. is fixed, the effective interest rate is now 1.01%, so we would say that interest rates (or yields) are trending down.

As another example, let's say China announces it will be selling all the Treasuries it currently holds. The markets would panic, and buyers of Treasuries would reduce the amount of money they would be willing to pay for them. Consequently, interest rates would skyrocket! The next day we find out it was just a nasty rumor, and that China actually wants to buy more U.S. Treasuries! Buyers would be out in force, paying more for the Treasuries, causing interest rates to fall.

The Treasury Department sells bonds in the open market for cash, from which it pays its expenses and interest to the bond holders.

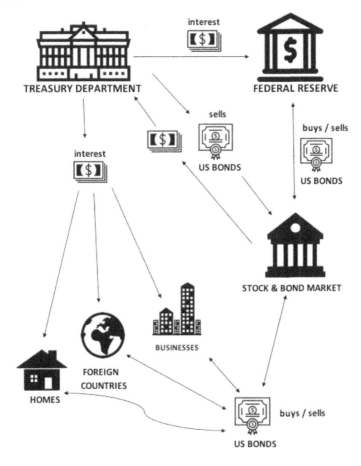

#3 Basically, all interest rates on car loans, mortgages, business loans, and savings, are pegged to the interest rates of Treasuries. Historically, Treasuries have been viewed as the strongest debt in the world. All other forms of debt are viewed as inferior and therefore carry a higher interest rate to compensate for added risk.

For example:

	Rating	Int. rate
US Treasuries	AAA	1.2%
30-year home mortgage	A	3.5%
Apple Inc.	AA+	2.0%
Car loan	B	6.0%
Pawn shop loan	F	200.0%

#4 This part is key—The Federal Reserve can effectively make interest rates go up or down by conducting open market buying or selling of mass quantities of Treasuries. When the Fed buys Treasuries, interest rates go down. When they are selling Treasuries, rates go up. The Fed can use this powerful tool to stimulate the economy by lowering rates or cooling an overheated economy by raising rates. Currently, the Fed is buying Treasuries to keep interest rates low in order to stimulate the weak economy that resulted from the Covid 19 pandemic.

Sound complicated? It is. Precision and timing of interest rate adjustments is critical. Imprecise adjustments, and an oil shortage in the late 1970's resulted in the highest inflation of modern times. Ignoring the warning signs in the housing and banking industries in 2008 resulted in the Great Recession.

In June 2021, the consumer price index rose by 5.4%, the highest move since 2008. As such, this puts the Fed in a box because they would rather be selling Treasuries in order to fight inflation. Instead, they are buying Treasuries in order to help the government pay its bills.

Who holds the government's debt?

It used to be that individuals and companies owned most of the nation's debt. The Fed has been so active buying Treasuries that it now owns 25% of the nation's debt:

(in trillions)

U.S. Individuals and companies	$6.9
Federal Reserve	7.3
China	1.2
Other foreign countries	7.0
U.S. Government agencies	5.7
Total national debt	$28.0

Something economists keep an eye on is the level of money in circulation. The Fed's open market activity has translated into printing money. If the money supply grows at an exceedingly fast rate, it tends to exacerbate the inflation problem. You can see from the following chart that the money supply has taken a giant leap in 2021.

For those of you who have never lived through a period of dramatic inflation, let me tell you about my experience. In 1981, the inflation rate was 10.3%. I bought a house and the interest rate on my mortgage was 18%. Inflation eventually retreated, but the economy faltered, and I laid awake at night trying to figure out how to make my mortgage payment if I lost my job.

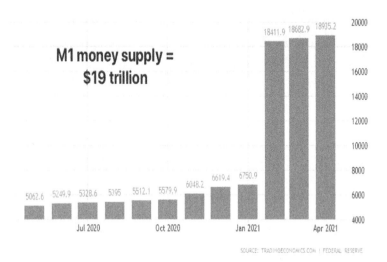

M1 money supply = $19 trillion

What our leaders have to say about our government's financial situation

Steve Mnuchin, Treasury Secretary under Donald Trump, pointed out in the government's 2020 fiscal year report, that the current financial situation is on an "unsustainable path".

Jerome Powell is Chairman of the Federal Reserve. On April 14, 2021, Mr. Powell spoke before the Economic Club in Washington. The following is paraphrased from his speech: US government borrowing is on an

<u>unsustainable path,</u> but the current debt level is very sustainable, and the government will have no problem making interest payments on time. The debt is growing meaningfully faster than the economy and that's unsustainable over time. The debt might fuel inflation but there should be no hurry to tackle the problem. This is not the time to prioritize that concern, but it is nonetheless an important concern when the economy is strong.

Janet Yellen is the Treasury Secretary. Here are some of her comments from the G7 meeting in June 2021."Most countries have fiscal space, and have the ability to put in place fiscal policies that will continue promoting recovery and deal with some of the long run challenges that all of us face when it comes to climate change and inclusive and sustainable growth, and we urge countries to do that," Yellen said inflation will remain elevated at 3% on a year-over-year basis until about the end of 2021."I personally believe that this represents transitory factors," she said. "We'll watch this very carefully, keep an eye on it and try to address issues that arise if it turns out to be necessary," Yellen said.

Yellen also said that President Joe Biden's fiscal 2022 spending budget of $6 trillion will push U.S. debt above the size of the U.S. economy, but will not contribute to inflationary pressures, which she views as temporary. "The recent inflation we have seen will be temporary, it's not something that's endemic," she said.

Ms. Yellen asked a Senate appropriations committee to approve billions in funding for the Treasury Department to support components of the $1.9 trillion American Rescue Plan, "In order for relief dollars to effectively reach their intended targets, we have to stand up and manage new federal programs"

Larry Summers is a world-renowned economist, Chief Economist of the World Bank, Treasury Secretary under President Clinton, director of the National Economic Council for President Obama, and was formerly President of Harvard University. Mr. Summers is sharply critical of the current excessive fiscal stimulus program and the Federal Reserve's loose money policies. He accuses the Fed of creating a "dangerous complacency" in financial markets and misreading the economy. He added that, "Data are pointing more toward higher inflation than I expected, and sooner." Mr. Summers pointed out that when the Fed starts to raise interest rates, "… that jolt will do real damage to financial stability and may do real damage to the economy".

Jamie Dimon is the CEO of JPMorgan Chase. In June 2021, Mr. Dimon, speaking at a banking conference, said he expects to see higher interest rates and more inflation.

Something to think about…..In the next recession, policymakers will rely on a combination of increased government spending and Federal Reserve money-printing to stimulate their way out of the downturn.

Let's pray that the economy strengthens over time because we are tapped out on stimulative programs. With the national debt in juggernaut-mode, more stimulus would most certainly cause inflation to spiral, and a significant devaluation of our currency.

SOCIAL SECURITY AND OTHER ENTITLMENTS

Here is the definition of government entitlements according to the U.S. Senate:

A Federal program or provision of law that requires payments to any person or unit of government that meets the eligibility criteria established by law. Entitlements constitute a binding obligation on the part of the Federal Government, and eligible recipients have legal recourse if the obligation is not fulfilled. Social Security and veterans' compensation and pensions are examples of entitlement programs.

These entitlements are long-term in nature because they are designated primarily for payment to people over the course of their future lives. As you can imagine, the estimated future cost of these commitments is enormous.

There are a number of public service non-profit organizations that periodically compute what they think is the true cost of these long-term commitments. Truth in Accounting (TIA) was founded in 2002 to "Compel governments to produce financial reports that are understandable, reliable, transparent and correct." TIA is a nonpartisan, non-profit organization with headquarters in Chicago. TIA calculated the unfunded cost of the governments future entitlements to be $96 trillion. (This figure is consistent with other forecasts I have seen). Add this to the $28 trillion of national debt and the total of all liabilities, funded and unfunded, is $124 trillion; or $375,000 per person in the U.S.

Steve Mnuchin, former Treasury Secretary, pointed out that the current financial situation with Social Security is on an "unsustainable path". As of now, it is expected to run out of funding in 2037, "…unless changes are made soon". The report also indicates that a solution may be the reduction of benefits, an increase in withholdings, or both.

This gloomy outlook is not really news. Most people sort of understand there is a problem but may not know the magnitude. Given the situation, can we really trust our government to come forth with a reasonable solution that will fulfill its legal obligation? Answer: NO.

Some typical government hypocrisy

The Employee Retirement Income Security Act of 1974 (ERISA) protects the interests of participants and beneficiaries in private-sector employee benefit plans. ERISA dictates that adequate money needs to be set aside to pay future pension obligations. It requires plans to inform participants of their rights under the plan and of the plan's financial status, and it gives plan participants the right to sue to recover benefits they have earned under the plan. ERISA also established the

Pension Benefit Guaranty Corporation to ensure that plan participants receive promised benefits in the event a pension plan fails for any reason.

In 1986, Congress created the Federal Employee Retirement System (FERS), which provides benefits for Congress and other federal employees. By law, FERS must be fully funded.

It's pure hypocrisy that Congress requires private sector retirement plans and FERS to be funded, yet Social Security is in trouble. This simply provides more evidence that Washington is not worthy of our trust. More reason we must be successful with an Article V resolution. We cannot allow Washington to default on the legal commitments it made to *We the People.*

'Means testing' is something that can help with the unfunded entitlements problem. Means testing is a way to determine if someone is eligible for help from the government, based upon whether that individual or family possesses the means to do without that help. The real estate billionaire Sam Zell made an interesting comment on CNBC: "I received a social security check in the mail. I didn't really think I should keep it, so I was going to send it back to the government since they need it more than I do. Then I thought; the government would just waste it, so I sent the check to my favorite charity."

IN PURSUIT OF A BALANCED BUDGET

"Mr. President, I rise today to talk about America's debt problem. The fact that we are here today to debate raising America's debt limit is a sign of leadership failure. It is a sign that the US government can't pay its own bills. It is a sign that we now depend on ongoing financial assistance from foreign countries to finance our government's reckless fiscal policies. Over the past five years, our federal debt has increased by $3.5 trillion to $8.6 trillion. That is "trillion" with a "T." That is money that we have borrowed from the Social Security trust fund, borrowed from China and Japan, borrowed from American taxpayers."

Since Senator Obama made that speech in March 2006, the federal debt has increased by $19.4 trillion (or 225%) to $28.0 trillion.

How the times have changed! An attitude of questioning the level of debt has gone to one of approving bills for expenditures in the trillions of dollars. Our federal government is so deep in debt that it's obvious this insanity must stop.

The following chart shows taxes versus spending from 2016 through 2026. There's a consistent pattern of spending more than is taken in, which is an unsustainable path.

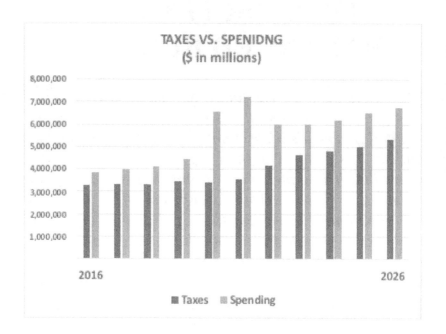

TAXES VS. SPENIDNG
($ in millions)

■ Taxes ■ Spending

I did some financial modeling of the government's operations to see how soon the government might be able to reach a balanced budget, assuming passage and implementation of Article V. We would all like to see a balanced budget right away, but since the infrastructure of the federal government is so wide, and deep, and the unmitigated out-of-control spending has been going on for so long, achieving a balanced budget will be like trying to make a 180-degree U-turn with an ocean liner.

I started my modeling with the six-year forecast developed by the White House's Office of Management and Budget ('OMB') as a base line. It shows a continuation of massive yearly deficits through 2026. This is what I call the "do nothing scenario", otherwise known as PLAN-A. It assumes our efforts with Article V were NOT successful so that we have to continue with the march to financial Armageddon.

PLAN-B assumes that we pass Article V in 2021 and the federal government miraculously balances the budget in 2022. I know this is not going to happen, but I just wanted to see what the best possible scenario would look like.

With PLAN-C, I assumed Article V would pass, and that the government would work hard to achieve a balanced budget by 2026 through aggressive reduction of operating expenses. Here is a summary of the three scenarios:

FORECAST SCENARIOS
FOR THE SIX YEARS (CUMULATIVE) 2022 through 2026
(in millions)

	PLAN-A	PLAN-B	PLAN-C
Tax revenue	$ 27,593,700	$ 27,593,700	$ 27,593,700
Sales of land	-	125,000	100,000
Total revneue	27,593,700	27,718,700	27,693,700
Operating expenses	(34,230,427)	(27,661,655)	(31,022,242)
Interest expense	(3,539,174)	(2,781,246)	(3,108,359)
Infrastructure payments	(1,000,000)	(1,000,000)	(1,000,000)
Total expenditures	(38,769,601)	(31,442,901)	(35,130,601)
Accumulated deficits	$ (11,175,901)	$ (3,724,201)	$ (7,436,901)
Year end national debt	$ (38,409,901)	$ (30,958,201)	$ (34,670,901)

(You can see the detailed forecasts at Appendix II.)

As you can see, even under the best possible scenario (PLAN-B), we will still be carrying well over $30 trillion in debt with annual interest payments of $464 billion. With PLAN-A, annual interest payments will grow to about $768 billion by 2026.

The OMB needs to develop a twenty-year plan that includes a substantial pay down of the principal debt balance. In other words, we need to do more than just achieve a balanced budget. We need to develop a repayment plan, just like someone who has too much credit card debt.

Things to note:
- In each of the projections I used the OMB's projected revenue, although it is highly probable the government will be aggressively increasing taxes over time. Also, I did not factor in the probability that increased taxes will likely reduce GDP.
- For PLAN-B and PLAN-C, I assumed the government would sell some of its land assets to help offset expenses.
- Interest expense fluctuates based on the level of debt, which is based on the level of deficits that need to be funded. Market perception of the government's stability affects interest rates and I assumed that PLAN-A will result in increasingly higher rates.
- If we go with PLAN-A (status quo, do nothing) it's highly likely U.S. Treasuries will be

downgraded by Standard and Poor's, and Moody's resulting in a rush to sell Treasuries in the open market—the consequence of which is higher interest rates, higher inflation, a collapse of the stock and bond markets, and a recession (or depression). However, I did not factor such a crisis into my projections.

This is not a pretty picture and shows the consequence of waiting way too long to take remedial action. Congress has been talking about a balanced budget for as long as I can remember but refuses to do anything about it. This is what I call brinksmanship; taking our freedom and lifestyle to the brink of destruction.

THE STATES NEED TO TAKE BACK THEIR POWER!

When I was a young man in high school, I remember Washington DC being this sort of faraway place where there was a lot of good history of the founders and how courageous they were in leading this new country. I felt secure that Washington would firmly deal with any adversaries who would encroach on our liberty. It was a sacred place where so much good had happened over the years. The president, Congress, and the Supreme Court were highly respected people who we could count on to resolve national issues. I had this comforting sense that Washington was powerful, and helpful.

Let's look back for a moment at some of the great things the government has achieved in the distant past:

- Our federal government created the conditions that have allowed private citizens and companies to build a great nation through capitalism and fruits of hard work.
- From the Land Ordinance of 1785 right on to the Homestead Act of 1862, the government offered cheap or free land to poor, hard-working people—a stake in their country.
- Educating everybody by offering free and universal public schools.

- Helping us retire with dignity. Social Security and Medicare keep millions of Americans out of poverty.
- Improving public health. The greatest advances in longevity are due to public sanitation measures such as water treatment, sewer systems and trash disposal.
- Building our transportation networks. Almost all U.S. highways and airports have been built with public money.
- Investing in communications. Creation of communications networks including the Post Office, telegraph, first transatlantic cable, and communication satellites. The internet was invented by the Defense Department—not Al Gore!
- Building our energy supply. Most energy investment comes from private companies, but the government has played a role.
- The space program and defense research continue to spin off benefits to our economy.
- Defending our freedom. The United States has faced serious threats of fascism and communism in its 245 years of independence, including two world wars, Korea, Vietnam and the Middle East.

About ten years ago, my wife LeeLee and I went to the Congressional Country Club in Bethesda Maryland to watch our great nephew, Beau Hossler, play as an amateur in the U.S. Open. In connection with the trip, we took a tour of Washington DC, including the Lincoln Memorial, the Jefferson Memorial, Vietnam War Memorial, Iwo Jima Memorial, Arlington Cemetery, and the Marine Corps War Memorial. It's quite moving to think of all that has been given to us by the Founders and those who paid the ultimate price for our freedom. A sense of incredible pride wells up inside as you realize what a blessing it is to be an American.

At the end of the tour, while I was experiencing these prideful emotions, another emotion started to creep into this wonderful moment. It was anger. Anger at Washington politicians who would speak of patriotism while trying to undermine the freedoms that we have so dearly embraced. The next emotion was one of embarrassment; that I was part of the generation who messed things up. Alas, here we are today with a gigantic, dysfunctional government that continues to impose more rules and regulations, more government programs, and out-of-control spending, that endangers our way of life. Today Washington is, to a large degree, a misguided enemy of the people. They are arrogant, self-righteous, and out of touch with reality. And as a retired finance professional, I am horrified at how they waste money and have no sense of accountability.

Are you fed up?

Rick Perry is a former governor of Texas, and he served as the Secretary of Energy from 2017 to 2019. He wrote a great book titled *FedUp!* which clearly makes the argument that we must step up and retake the reins of our government that has abused our trust. He said, "The simple answer is this: Americans want to live free. They want to gather with people of common beliefs and goals. To establish communities in which they can prosper. They do not want to be told how to live their lives. They certainly don't want some faraway bureaucrat, judge, or representative of a different community telling them how to live. That liberty has been the essence of America ever since the colonists came here".

The border wall fiasco

This is another story that shows just how dysfunctional our federal government is. Our country has had significant issues with the southern border for a long time. Congress has been unable and unwilling to come up with a solution, so President Trump went around them and found a way to get $10 billion from the Defense Department to build a wall. When Mr. Biden took office, he quickly put an end to construction of the wall. While the wall contractors have discontinued work, they have thus far received $2 billion in work cancellation fees.

There was 450 miles of wall construction that had been competed at the Arizona border, but none in Texas. Illegal immigration continues and is at a 20-year high number of migrants crossing our open border. Since border security is one of the top issues facing the state of Texas, Governor Gregg Abbott is trying to pick up where President Trump left off. Abbott has announced a plan for Texas to build its own border wall and arrest migrants who attempt to scale it. But given the litany of practical and legal concerns that could hold up the project — from fundraising to seizing private property to the limited powers of state government over immigration — it's unclear if he'll actually be able to do it.

In the Constitution, you will find that one of the principal things the federal government is supposed to do is guard the borders of our country. Without borders, you no longer have a country! The Constitution also states that the consideration of laws and federal projects shall be approved through an orderly process that includes Congress and the President.

In the case of the Mexican border, it's obvious Congress is not capable of coming up with a solution to guard our borders. Governor Abbott must guard his state's southern border without the help of Washington DC. This is just more evidence that our federal government needs to be reconstructed through an Article V convention of states.

What our Founders intended

The most celebrated form of government in the world is democracy. It's a system of, by, and for the people. However, democracy is susceptible to human frailties that afflict us all—greed, prejudice, hubris, intellectual dishonesty, and moral weakness.

In order to help convince their fellow Americans of their view that the Constitution would help preserve democracy, and not threaten freedom, James Madison, Alexander Hamilton, and John Jay teamed up in 1788 to write a series of essays in defense of the Constitution. The essays, which appeared in newspapers addressed to the people of the state of New York, are known as the Federalist Papers. They are regarded as one of the most authoritative sources on the meaning of the Constitution, including constitutional principles such as checks and balances, federalism, and separation of powers.

James Madison, who is generally regarded as the Father of the Constitution, when arguing for its ratification in Federalist #45 wrote this: "The powers delegated by the proposed Constitution to the federal government are few and defined. Those which are to remain in the state governments are numerous and indefinite. The former will be exercised principally on external objects, as war, peace, negotiation, and foreign commerce; and which last the power of taxation will for the most part be connected. The powers reserved to the several states will extend to all objects which, in the ordinary course of affairs, concern the lives, liberties, and properties of the people, and the internal order, improvement, and prosperity of the State. The operations of the Federal Government will be most extensive and important in times of war and danger; those of the state governments, in times of peace and security".

Thomas Jefferson, the primary draftsman of the Declaration of Independence, admonished Americans; "When governments fear the people, there is liberty. When the people fear the government, there is tyranny. The strongest reason for the people to retain the right to keep and bear arms is, as a last resort, to protect themselves against tyranny in government."

Here is another quote from Rick Perry that I like: "While the national government was intentionally strong when it came to foreign and war powers, its domestic authority was greatly limited, leaving ample room for the states to be the hub of American self-government. By the will of the people, our government exists to guarantee our right to live according to the dictates of our conscience, to chart the direction for our lives, and to join with like-minded people to journey down that path. States are the vehicles by which we can do that. States not only matter; they serve as the core of the great American experiment".

The term 'like-minded people' says that we are free to live in any state we desire in order to live with a local government that sees life in America most closely to what we want. One of the beauties of our country is that we are free to choose to move from state to state and live anywhere our heart desires. I lived in California for 50 years and loved it. We now live in Arkansas and love it as well.

No hope for the current federal government

We have a Congress that is totally dysfunctional. The two parties hate each other. Many of the members vilify, lie about, and defame the other party's members. Congress is run by representatives whose goal in life is to gain more and more power.

If our government leaders told us they were going to work on a balanced budget, would you believe it? If they said the two parties had agreed on a balanced budget amendment, do you believe it would be implemented? I wouldn't believe it either. I don't think that even a financial crisis would be enough to get Congress to agree on a balanced budget amendment. After all, they've had plenty of time to deal with it, and the finances are only getting worse.

Congress knows Social Security and other entitlements are at risk, but they haven't provided a solution. If the federal government was a private sector corporation, it would be filing for bankruptcy. Instead, the Federal Reserve is bailing them out by printing money.

On a positive note, there are a number of federal and state representatives, former and current, who publicly support a reduction in federal government powers via Article V. Let's encourage them to keep working with *We the People* to do what is necessary to save our democracy. It's especially important that you contact members of your state's congress and tell them you are expecting them to vote in favor of a Convention of States, and for ratification of an Article V amendment to our Constitution.

PROCESS FOR A CONVENTION OF STATES UNDER ARTICLE V

At this point, I hope you will agree that we need big changes in federal government functions;

1.) A balanced budget
2.) Term limits on elected representatives
3.) Limited power and jurisdiction

Here are the basic steps:

- The 50 states' legislators need to debate the issues and get the approval of both chambers (house and senate).
- It takes 34 states (2/3) to call for a Convention of States under Article V.
- During the Convention, amendments would be drafted and agreed to.
- The final process involves all 50 states voting on the proposed amendments. If 38 states (3/4) vote in favor, the U.S. Constitution will be thus amended.

The U.S. Congress has no vote on this matter and will be charged with effecting the changes as directed by the amended Constitution.

What might our federal government look like if the proposed amendments to our Constitution are ratified?

There will be a great deal of work to achieve a balanced

budget. I suppose term limits will be phased in. I suspect the most debated issue at the convention would be the determination as to what the role of our future federal government should be. It may well be limited to what the founders originally planned in Article 1, Section 8 of the Constitution:

- To levy income and import taxes
- Coin money
- Regulate commerce
- Defense
- The Post Office and Patent Office (although it might be better to privatize them)
- Borrow money on the credit of the U.S.
- While not in the Constitution, it might make sense to have Washington continue to manage Social Security and other entitlement programs.

Other restrictions that might be proposed at the convention include:

- Require Members of Congress to live under the same laws they pass for the rest of us.
- Get the federal government out of our healthcare system.
- Get the federal government out of our education system.
- Stop unelected federal bureaucrats from imposing regulations.

So, what are the arguments against an Article V convention?

- Uncertainty and potential for unintended consequences. Fear of the unknown.
- Unanswered questions about the rules and process that would govern a convention.
- The biggest concern raised is the possibility of a "runaway convention" where delegates start proposing unrelated amendments, or even a complete rewriting of the Constitution.

Robert Kelly is an attorney and Staff Counsel for the Convention of States Action ('COSA') organization and has researched the runaway convention threat. In a nutshell, the text of Article V, the history and purpose behind it, plus Congress's own inaction, all indicate that an Article V convention can be limited to a particular topic or set of topics.

Our Founders knew what they were doing when they voted unanimously to put the convention provision in Article V. A convention is not some all-powerful body with authority to unilaterally scrap our Constitution, though convention opponents often represent it in that light. It is a limited-purpose committee intended to give the states the ability to propose particular amendments that Congress never would. As such, the state legislatures can impose binding subject-matter restraints on the convention to ensure that it does not run away.

Status of a Convention of States

15 states have sent a resolution to the U.S. Congress making application to call for a convention for amendment under Article V. (We need a total of 34 for passage). A total of 9 states have passed the resolution in one chamber; awaiting resolution from the other chamber. Another 6 states are in active hearings.

FILED COS RESOLUTON (49 STATES)	PASSED COMMITTEE HEARING (30 STATES)	PASSED LEGISLATIVE CHAMBER (24 STATES)	PASSED COS RESOLUTIC (15 STATES)
AK,AL,AR,AZ,CA,CO, DE,FL,GA,HI,ID,IL,IN, IA,KS,KY,LA,MA,MD, ME,MI,MN,MS,MO, MT,NE,NV,NH,NU, NM,NU,NC,ND,OH, OK,OR,PA,RI,SC,SD, TN,TX,UT,VA,VT,WA, WI,WV,WY	AK, AL, AR, AZ, FL, GA, IL, IN, IA,KS,LA,MI,MO, MS,NC,NEND,NH,NM, OK,PA,SC,SD,TN,TX,UT, VA,WI,WV,WY	AK, AL, AR, AZ, FL, GA, IN, IA, LA, MO, MS, NC, ND, NH, NM, OK, SC, SD, TN, TX, UT, VA, WI, WV	AK, AL, AR, AZ, FL,GA,IN, LA, MO, MS, ND, OK, TN TX, UT

How you can help

The Convention of States Action (COSA) is a non-profit, grass roots project and you can help spread the word by working on one or more of the following:
- Educating state legislators about Article V.
- Educating citizens about how to be self-governing and the advantages of less 'big government'.
- Helping prepare your state legislature for the Article V process.
- Contribute money to COSA to help get the word out.

- Speak at local community organizations about the dire need to invoke Article V.
- Spread the word through social media.

As Alan Simpson (retired Senator of Wyoming and Chair of the National Commission on Fiscal Responsibility and Reform) once said, ***"Learn to take part, or be taken apart"***.

Start by signing the petition at:
https://conventionofstates.com/take_action

Here is a partial list of government leaders who have advocated for a Convention of States:

Hon. Rick Perry	Rep. Ralph Norman
Rep. Jeff Duncan	Hon. Jason Chavetz
Hon. Ben Carson	Hon. Tom Coburn
Hon. Sarah Palin	Lt. Col. Allen West
Lt. Col. Bill Cowan	Gov. Greg Abbot
Rep. Williams Timmons	Hon. Jeb Bush
Sen. Marco Rubio	Hon. Jim DeMint
Hon. Mike Huckabee	Gov. Ron DeSantis
Hon.Bobby Jindal	Hon. Kenneth Cuccinelli

There are a number of books written over the last ten years that do an excellent job of shining a light on the many injustices of our current federal government. Here is a list that I recommend:

- The Deep State – Hon. Jason Chaffetz
- Why Government Fails So Often – Peter H. Schuck
- The Russia Hoax – Gregg Jarrett
- Now or Never – Hon. Jim DeMint
- Smashing the DC Monopoly – Hon. Tom Coburn
- The Liberty Amendments – Mark Levin
- The Healing of America – T.R. Reid
- FedUp! – Hon. Rick Perry
- Exonerated – Dan Bongino

APPENDIX I

UNITED STATES GOVERNMENT
STATEMENT OF OPERATIONS
Fiscal year ended September 30, 2020
(in billions of dollars)

REVENUE:

Individual Income Tax and Withholding Tax	$	2,855
Corporate Income Taxes		317
Excise Taxes		93
Unemployment Taxes		41
Customs Duties		66
Estate and Gift Taxes		18
Other Taxes and Receipts		166
Miscellaneous Revenue		27
TOTAL REVENUE		**3,583**
GOVERNEMENT OPERATING COSTS		7,412
NET OPERATING DEFICIT	$	(3,829)

UNITED STATES GOVERNMENT
BALANCE SHEET

As of September 30, 2020

(in billions of dollars)

ASSETS:

Cash and Other Monetary Assets	$	1,927
Accounts Receivable		321
Direct Loans and Guarantees Receivable		1,578
Inventories and Related Property		380
General Property, Plant, and Equipment		1,145
Securities and Investments		122
Investment in Special Purpose Vehicles		108
Investments in Government Sponsered Enterprises		109
Other Assets		261
TOTAL ASSETS	$	5,951

LIABILITIES:

Accounts Payable	$	105.0
Federal Debt and Interest Payable		21,083
Federal Employee and Veteran Benefits Payable		9,409
Environmental and Disposal Liabilities		603
Benefits Due and Payable		256
Loan Guarantee Liability		520
Insurance and Guarantee Program Liability		200
Other Liabilities		571
TOTAL LIABILITIES		32,747
LIABILITIES IN EXCESS OF ASSETS		(26,796)
TOTAL	$	5,951.0

UNITED STATES GOVERNMENT
COSTS AND EXPENSES BY DEPARTMENT
Fiscal year 2020
(in billions of dollars)

Department of Health and Human Services	$ 1,407.1
Social Security Administration	1,157.3
Department of Veterans Affairs	985.0
Department of Defense	745.0
Department of the Treasury	560.7
Small Business Administration	559.0
Department of Labor	493.2
Interest Expense on Treasury Securities	**371.1**
Department of Agriculture	187.9
Office of Personnel Management	162.0
Department of Education	156.9
Department of Homeland Security	113.6
Security Assistance Accounts	112.0
Department of Transportation	107.7
Department of Energy	55.5
Department of Justice	37.3
Department of Housing and Urban Development	34.1
Department of State	32.9
National Aeronautics and Space Administration	22.1
Department of the Interior	20.6
Department of Commerce	15.5
U.S. Agency for International Development	13.8
Federal Communications Commission	13.5
Railroad Retirement Board	13.1
Environmental Protection Agency	8.7
U.S. Postal Service	7.5
National Science Foundation	7.3
Smithsonian Institution	1.0
Millennium Challenge Corporation	0.6
Export-Import Bank of the U.S.	0.4
U.S. Nuclear Regulatory Commission	0.2
National Credit Union Administration	0.1
U.S. International Development Finance Corporation	(0.1)
Farm Credit System Insurance Corporation	(0.1)
General Services Administration	(0.5)
Securities and Exchange Commission	(1.1)
Tennessee Valley Authority	(1.3)
National Railroad Retirement Investment Trust	(1.7)
Pension Benefit Guaranty Corporation	(2.8)
Federal Deposit Insurance Corporation	(4.8)
All other entities	21.7
TOTAL	$7,412.00

APPENDIX II

PLAN - A

UNITED STATES GOVERNMENT
FORECASTED DEFICITS AND DEBT
AS CURRENTLY FORECASTED BY THE OMB
Fiscal years ending September 30,
(in millions)

	2021	2022	2023	2024	2025	2026	2021-2026
TAX RECEIPTS	$ 3,580,800	4,174,200	$ 4,641,000	$ 4,827,800	$ 5,037,900	5,332,000	$ 27,593,700
LAND SALES	0	0	0	0	0	0	0
TOTAL REVENUE	3,580,800	4,174,200	4,641,000	4,827,800	5,037,900	5,332,000	27,593,700
OPERATING EXPENSES	(6,841,460)	(5,310,821)	(5,271,561)	(5,391,001)	(5,638,411)	(5,777,173)	(34,230,427)
INTEREST EXPENSE	(463,541)	(500,279)	(541,439)	(595,799)	(669,289)	(768,827)	(3,539,174)
INFRASTRUCTURE PAYMENTS	0	(200,000)	(200,000)	(200,000)	(200,000)	(200,000)	(1,000,000)
TOTAL CASH EXPENDITURES	(7,305,001)	(6,011,100)	(6,013,000)	(6,186,800)	(6,507,700)	(6,746,000)	(38,769,601)
DEFICIT FOR THE CURRENT YEAR	$ (3,724,201)	(1,836,900)	$ (1,372,000)	$ (1,359,000)	$ (1,469,800)	(1,414,000)	$ (11,175,901)
NATIONAL DEBT - BEG. OF YEAR	$ (27,234,000)	(30,958,201)	$ (32,795,101)	$ (34,167,101)	$ (35,526,101)	(36,995,901)	
NATIONAL DEBT - END OF YEAR	$ (30,958,201)	(32,795,101)	$ (34,167,101)	$ (35,526,101)	$ (36,995,901)	(38,409,901)	

PLAN - B

UNITED STATES GOVERNMENT
FORECASTED DEFICITS AND DEBT
BALANCED BUDGET BY 2022

Fiscal years ending September 30,
(in millions)

	2021	2022	2023	2024	2025	2026	2021-2026
TAX RECEIPTS	$ 3,580,800	4,174,200	4,641,000	4,827,800	5,037,900	5,332,000	$ 27,593,700
LAND SALES	0	25,000	25,000	25,000	25,000	25,000	125,000
TOTAL REVENUE	3,580,800	4,199,200	4,666,000	4,852,800	5,062,900	5,357,000	27,718,700
OPERATING EXPENSES	(6,841,460)	(3,535,659)	(4,002,459)	(4,189,259)	(4,399,359)	(4,693,459)	(27,661,655)
INTEREST EXPENSE	(463,541)	(463,541)	(463,541)	(463,541)	(463,541)	(463,541)	(2,781,246)
INFRASTRUCTURE PAYMENTS	0	(200,000)	(200,000)	(200,000)	(200,000)	(200,000)	(1,000,000)
TOTAL CASH EXPENDITURES	(7,305,001)	(4,199,200)	(4,666,000)	(4,852,800)	(5,062,900)	(5,357,000)	(31,442,901)
DEFICIT FOR THE CURRENT YEAR	$ (3,724,201)	-	-	-	-	-	$ (3,724,201)
NATIONAL DEBT - BEG. OF YEAR	(27,234,000)	(30,958,201)	(30,958,201)	(30,958,201)	(30,958,201)	(30,958,201)	
NATIONAL DEBT - END OF YEAR	$ (30,958,201)	(30,958,201)	(30,958,201)	(30,958,201)	(30,958,201)	(30,958,201)	

PLAN - C

UNITED STATES GOVERNMENT
FORECASTED DEFICITS AND DEBT
BALANCED BUDGET BY 2026

Fiscal years ending September 30,
(in millions)

	2021	2022	2023	2024	2025	2026	2021-2026
TAX RECEIPTS	$ 3,580,800	4,174,200	4,641,000	4,827,800	5,037,900	5,332,000	27,593,700
LAND SALES	0	0	25,000	25,000	25,000	25,000	100,000
TOTAL REVENUE	3,580,800	4,174,200	4,666,000	4,852,800	5,062,900	5,357,000	27,693,700
OPERATING EXPENSES	(6,841,460)	(5,143,476)	(4,921,076)	(4,775,106)	(4,733,412)	(4,607,712)	(31,022,242)
INTEREST EXPENSE	(463,541)	(492,624)	(516,924)	(536,694)	(549,288)	(549,288)	(3,108,359)
INFRASTRUCTURE PAYMENTS	0	(200,000)	(200,000)	(200,000)	(200,000)	(200,000)	(1,000,000)
TOTAL CASH EXPENDITURES	(7,305,001)	(5,836,100)	(5,638,000)	(5,511,800)	(5,482,700)	(5,357,000)	(35,130,601)
DEFICIT FOR THE CURRENT YEAR	$ (3,724,201)	(1,661,900)	(972,000)	(659,000)	(419,800)	-	(7,436,901)
NATIONAL DEBT - BEG. OF YEAR	$ (27,234,000)	(30,958,201)	(32,620,101)	(33,592,101)	(34,251,101)	(34,670,901)	
NATIONAL DEBT - END OF YEAR	$ (30,958,201)	(32,620,101)	(33,592,101)	(34,251,101)	(34,670,901)	(34,670,901)	

APPENDIX III

COMPLETE TEXT OF ARTICLE V OF THE U.S. CONSTITUTION

THE CONGRESS, whenever two thirds of both Houses shall deem it necessary, shall propose Amendments to this Constitution, or on the Application of the Legislatures of two thirds of the several States, shall call a Convention for proposing Amendments, which, in either Case, shall be valid to all Intents and Purposes, as Part of this Constitution, when ratified by the Legislatures of three fourths of the several States, or by Conventions in three fourths thereof, as the one or the other Mode of Ratification may be proposed by the Congress; Provided that no Amendment which may be made prior to the Year One thousand eight hundred and eight shall in any Manner affect the first and fourth Clauses in the Ninth Section of the first Article; and that no State, without its Consent, shall be deprived of its equal Suffrage in the Senate.

[all proceeds from sales of this booklet go to: Convention of States Action]

Made in the USA
Monee, IL
21 August 2021

75443021R00049